HERCULES

THE LEGENDARY JOURNEYS™

SCRAPBOOK

by Marie Morreale
Hercules is based on the Universal Television series
created by Christian Williams

SCHOLASTIC INC.

New York   Toronto   London   Auckland   Sydney

ISBN 0-590-87104-8

12 11 10 9 8 7 6 5 4 3 2   6 7 8 9/9 0 1/0

Printed in the U.S.A.   09
First Scholastic printing, June 1996

Meet
HERCULES
the greatest hero of all time.

Hercules is son of the god Zeus and a mortal woman named Alcmene. He possesses a strength the world has never seen. Hercules journeys the earth, battling the evil monsters and creatures who are followers of his wicked stepmother Hera, the all-powerful Queen of the gods. Wherever there is evil, wherever the poor, the weak, the innocent suffer, there is Hercules, the greatest hero of all time.

Xena™

The Princess Warrior Xena was once Hercules' mortal enemy, determined to destroy him. But Hercules changed all that and turned her to the path of good and glory. Though haunted by her wicked past, Xena courageously battles villains and protects the innocent from the forces of evil.

Iolaus™

Iolaus is Hercules' sidekick and best friend. He is fast and tough and is always there when Hercules needs him.

The Seer™

His eyes may be blind, but his heart sees all. Unfortunately The Seer always predicts doom and gloom, so when he appears on the scene, get ready for disaster!

Salmoneus™

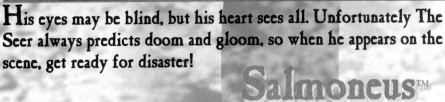

Sly as a fox, Salmoneus would rather bargain his way out of a sticky situation. But when push comes to shove, he will fight alongside his friend, Hercules.

Hercules and the Lost Kingdom

As protector of the innocent and weak, Hercules battles and defeats the 20-foot-tall Gargan the Giant.

Before Hercules can rest from his battle with Gargan, messengers from the city of Troy beg him to return with them and free them from a horrible curse placed on them by the goddess Hera. As Hercules sets off for Troy, he comes across the beautiful Deianeira. She has been captured by enemies and is about to be sacrificed to the gods!

Hercules saves Deianeira and she accompanies him on his journey. But along the way, they are attacked by a mysterious Blue Priest who calls up a huge sea monster to swallow up Hercules and Deianeira. In the belly of the beast, Hercules mightily fights and he and Deianeira are freed.

Once again Hercules and Deianeira head for Troy. This time they meet up with Ilus, King of Troy, and his men. They have escaped from an evil army known as the Blue Monks who have taken over Troy. Just before Hercules leads them into battle with the Blue Monks, King Ilus, who is dying, reveals that Deianeira is really his long-lost daughter.

In hopes of saving the people of Troy, Deianeira slips out of the camp and surrenders herself to the Blue Priest, leader of the Blue Monks.

But when Hercules and the citizens of Troy realize what Deianeira has done, they attack the Blue Monks. Hercules slays the Blue Priest and the evil monks are defeated. Deianeira thanks him for all he has done to help Troy and she takes her rightful place as leader of her people. As Hercules bids farewell, he has no idea that he and Deianeira will meet once again for an even darker adventure!

Hercules and the Circle of Fire

Hercules searches for a cure to heal the wound of his friend Cheiron, a satyr (part man, part goat). Hercules finds the cure—in the form of a potion from a magic fountain—but it fails to cure his friend.

Meanwhile Hera, Hercules' stepmother and Queen of the gods, is up to her evil tricks again. This time she has caused an icy wind to blow that will extinguish all the fires throughout the earth.

Hercules goes on a quest to save the world from the deep freeze. Along the way he once again meets the beautiful Deianeira, who has gone to the Temple of Hera to plead for fire to save the people of Troy. When that doesn't work, she accompanies Hercules on his journey.

Hercules and Deianeira head for the palace of the immortal keeper of fire, Prometheus. But he, too, is affected by the chill of Hera. Though he is almost frozen solid, he whispers to Hercules that Hera has stolen the Eternal Torch in an attempt to destroy the people of earth.

As the world slips into a deep freeze, Hercules and Deianeira journey to find the Eternal Torch Hera has stolen. Along the way they must battle giants and witches that Hera has sent to defeat them.

Hercules must use all of his strength to combat the monsters of Hera.

Risking his own life, Hercules finds the Eternal Torch and restores fire to earth. When Hercules returns home, he lights a circle of fire around his ailing friend Cheiron. When the fire dies down, Cheiron's wounds have been healed and he has been transformed from a satyr to a mortal man.

Hercules *in the* Underworld

A beautiful young woman named Iole arrives at the home of Hercules and Deianeira (who is now Hercules' wife) to ask for their help. A black hole to the underworld has opened up near Iole's village. Evil spirits and dangerous fumes escaping from the hole threaten the lives of the villagers, and Iole begs Hercules to return with her to close up the hole.

Meanwhile ...

Hercules asks the centaur Nessus to protect Deianeira while he goes on his journey. But Nessus really is one of Hera's creatures and is jealous of Hercules. As Hercules leaves, Nessus tries to hurt Deianeira. Luckily Hercules hears her cries and turns back and saves Deianeira.

Once Hercules and Iole finally arrive at her village, the hero enters the black hole to the Underworld.

In the Underworld, Hercules meets Charon the Boatman. He tells Hercules that chaos and danger are everywhere because Cerberus, the three-headed dog that guards the gates to the Underworld, is on the loose.

Hercules finds Cerberus and the dog attacks! But Hercules is able to calm the dog down, collar him, and return him to his rightful place at the gates of the Underworld. As Hercules returns to earth, the black hole disappears and all is back to normal.

Hercules in the Maze of the MINOTAUR

One day, Andius and Danion, two brothers from the town Alturia, come to visit Hercules. They tell him about a terrible monster they had mistakenly released from its cave. Once freed, the creature had attacked and nearly killed them! Hercules and his friend Iolaus go with the two brothers back to their town in search of the monster. However, when Hercules and Iolaus arrive in town, they find that no one, except the brothers, believes there is a monster.

But there *is* a monster. He is a Minotaur, a raging beast who once was a handsome man and deceived all those he met. The god Zeus cursed him and turned him into the ugliest of all creatures. The Minotaur was banished to live imprisoned in underground caves . . . until Andius and Danion let him loose. Just as Hercules is about to return home, the Minotaur tunnels underneath the village and drags Iolaus to his lair.

Hercules and a small band of men from Alturia follow the Minotaur and Iolaus. After wandering through a maze of underground tunnels, Hercules finds the hideous creature with the body of a man and the head of a bull—the Minotaur!

A raging battle echoes throughout the underground tunnels. And just as Hercules is about to strike a fatal blow to the Minotaur, the creature cries out, "Would you really kill your brother?"

Stunned by the question, Hercules lowers his sword. But then, the Minotaur turns and attacks the terrorized Iolaus. To save his friend, Hercules leaps at the Minotaur, kicks at him backwards, and the creature falls into a jagged rock. Zeus appears and tells Hercules that the Minotaur was really his monstrous brother Gryphus and now the world is finally free of the evil he caused.

The Wrong Path

The Wrong Path

Hercules is grief stricken. The goddess Hera, his stepmother, has destroyed his family—his wife Deianeira and their three children. In revenge, Hercules vows to follow a new path, a path of destruction. His first mission is to destroy all the temples of Hera. But when he storms the first hall of worship to the goddess, he finds a beautiful slave girl, Aegina, about to be sacrificed. At that moment, Hercules realizes he is on the wrong path and he returns to his senses and rescues Aegina!

Back on the road of truth and goodness, Hercules and Aegina travel to the town of Ister, where a she-demon is turning the farmers into stone. Hercules swears he will challenge the serpentlike demon face-to-face and enters her cave of darkness.

Immediately he is confronted by the she-demon and all of Hercules' powers are tested. Just as she whips her lethal tail around Hercules, he is able to slip out of her slimy grasp!

With one last burst of strength, Hercules dodges a swipe of the she-demon's tail. In all the confusion, the creature whips her tail back onto herself and in seconds she is turned to stone! Once again, Hercules has conquered evil and once again he travels the path of the just and good.

The Road to Calydon

A group of war-weary soldiers and their families are led by a man named Broteas. They are searching for a safe place to settle when they come across the ghost town of Parthus. Taking refuge against a raging storm in the deserted village, they go to sleep as night falls. The next morning, the travelers discover their food has gone bad and their water has turned to blood. Just

then Hercules and The Seer come upon the frightened group. The Seer tells them that the town of Parthus has been cursed by Hera and urges them all to leave.

As Hercules leads the travelers away from the cursed town, trouble follows them. They are caught in a terrible rock storm, but Hercules protects the group, including the kind and lovely Jana and the orphan Ixion.

Hera is determined to destroy Hercules and his friends and she sends monstrous bounty hunters to attack them! But once again Hercules wins the battle.

Hercules and the band must travel across the dangerous Stymphalian swamp. There they are attacked by a huge flying dinosaur. But Hercules saves the day and the tired travelers find the road to safety.

Eye of the Beholder

Hercules learns that a village is in desperate trouble. Their water supply is being stolen by the evil Hera. A giant Cyclops is diverting the water to one of Hera's vineyards. Anyone who gets too close to the vineyard is attacked by the Cyclops. As Hercules heads toward the vineyards, he discovers a traveling toga salesman named Salmoneus, who had been hurled into the trees by the Cyclops.

When Hercules confronts the Cyclops, our hero realizes the Cyclops can only see straight ahead. So he attacks him from the side. Once Hercules subdues the monster, he asks the Cyclops why he's so angry and fearsome. "Because I'm so ugly," the Cyclops answers. He explains that the villagers have persecuted him because they were afraid of his looks.

When the villagers learn that Hercules has spared the Cyclops' life, they become angry. When they see the giant Cyclops, they begin to stone him. Hercules quickly stops the angry mob, explains that the Cyclops is really their friend, and convinces them all to live together in peace.

The Gladiator

Menas Maxius and his wife Postera are wealthy but evil citizens of Apropus. They capture innocent people and turn them into slaves. They force the slaves to become Gladiators and fight wild beasts for their amusement. One of the Gladiators is Gladius.

When Gladius was captured his wife Felicita escaped. After many months of searching, she finds Hercules and asks for his help to free Gladius.

In order to find Gladius, Hercules and Iolaus get captured by Menas' men. Once they are inside, they are groomed to be Gladiators, too. At the same time, Felicita is found lurking outside the prison and Menas and Postera come up with a devilish plan!

The evil couple take Iolaus and Felicita and bind and gag them. Unless Hercules and Gladius fight, Menas and Postera threaten they will kill their hostages.

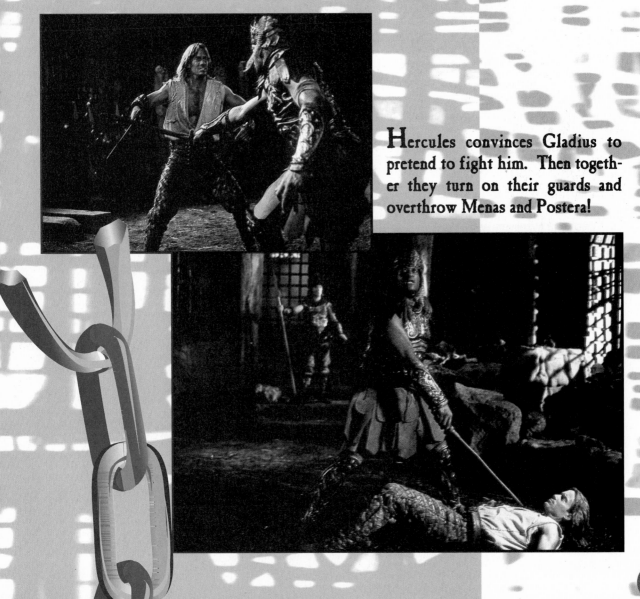

Hercules convinces Gladius to pretend to fight him. Then together they turn on their guards and overthrow Menas and Postera!

Hercules and the Amazon Women

Hercules journeys home to celebrate the wedding of Iolaus. But on the way they are attacked by the monstrous, multiheaded Hydra, a creature sent by his evil stepmother, the goddess Hera. The poisonous powers of the Hydra are no match for Hercules. He slays the serpent and continues on his way.

Before the wedding can take place, Hercules and Iolaus are summoned to aid a village being attacked by unseen monsters. When the brave friends go to investigate, they are attacked by savage Amazon women warriors. Iolaus is slain and Hercules is taken prisoner.

Hercules doesn't stay captive long and escapes from the Amazons. Angry that Hercules escaped, Hera tricks Hercules into fighting more of her evil creatures.

Hera orders Hippolyta, Queen of the Amazons, to kill Hercules, but she refuses. Hera takes possession of Hippolyta's body and leads an attack against Hercules and the men slaves of the Amazon women. But Hercules will not take arms against Hippolyta and in a rage, Hera throws the beautiful warrior over a cliff. A sad Hercules carries the body of Hippolyta back to her village and demands that his father, the god Zeus, change what has happened to Iolaus and Hippolyta.

HERCULES
the greatest hero of all time.

Hercules' journeys continue on. He will always use his super-human strength to right the wrongs and save the innocent!